KEYS TO
DISCOVERING
GOD'S
WILL

Dale A. O'Shields

Keys to Discovering God's Will
© 2005 by Dale A. O'Shields

Published by Life Change Resources
Gaithersburg, MD
www.lifechangeresources.com

Unless otherwise noted all Scripture quotations are taken from the *New Living Translation*. Scripture quotations marked NIV are from the *New International Version*, © 1960, 1962, 1963, 1968, 1971, 1972, 1973, 1975, 1977, 1995 by the Lockman Foundation. Used by permission. Scripture quotations marked TEV are taken from the *Today's English Version*, Second Edition, Copyright © 1992 by American Bible Society. Used by permission.

ISBN 0-9766566-1-2

Second Printing February 2005

Printed in the United States of America

Printing: Graphic Visions, Gaithersburg, MD

Getting Started
On The Journey

One of the challenges most Christian believers face at some point in their spiritual journey involves discovering God's will. How do we really know what God wants us to do with our lives? How can we be sure that we are doing God's will?

It helps to know that God's will is discoverable. Throughout the Bible we find examples of people seeking and finding the will of God. From the study of biblical characters, and from reviewing the experiences of Christian believers over the centuries, we too can learn and apply a practical process for finding out what God wants us to:

- Be
- Do

These two words are important. God's will first involves who we are becoming—the growth of our character—and secondarily, what we are doing with our lives.

I am convinced from Scripture that, if we are becoming the person God wants us to be— growing in Christ-like character and actively moving forward toward spiritual maturity—we can be sure that God will help us discover what He wants us to do.

All too often the emphasis of finding God's will is focused on the "doing" part, instead of the "being" part. The Bible makes it clear that the impact and fruitfulness of our lives is determined by issues of our heart and character, not our profession or occupation, or geographic location. God's greatest concern for you and me is, "What kind of person are we becoming?"

Take a look at the following verses:

> "Trust in the LORD with all your heart;
> do not depend on your own understanding.
> Seek his will in all you do, and he will direct
> your paths" *(Proverbs 3:5-6)*.

> "If you keep yourself pure, you will be a
> utensil God can use for his purpose.
> Your life will be clean, and you will be
> ready for the Master to use you for every
> good work" *(II Timothy 2:21)*.

Both of these passages focus on issues of heart and character. As we stay connected to God and grow in His grace, He promises to direct our paths and guide us into the good work He has ordained for us.

Pursuing God's will is the greatest and wisest thing we can do. His will is the best for us because:

God is able to see the end from the beginning.

He knows where life decisions take us. As the all-wise God, He sees the potential "dead ends" of life that we cannot see. He also knows the avenues that will open up phenomenal opportunities for our growth and fruitfulness.

God is able to help us function as He created us to function.

God designed us. He understands our unique make-up, our personality, our strengths and weaknesses. Living in God's will allows us to function as God created us to function.

▣ God is able to guide us to the fulfillment of our highest purpose.

Sadly, many people never live out their highest purpose. They settle for a comfortable life, a status quo existence and risk-free pathways. While they may do good things, they never experience the best God has for them. Living in God's will allows us to move beyond an ordinary purpose to an extraordinary purpose, from the motivation of earthly rewards to the inspiration of living for eternal rewards.

▣ God is able to remove from us the impurities and negative influences that destroy us.

When we get into God's will we are positioned for purification. All of us have impurities in us and negative influences around us that restrict our spiritual, emotional and relational health and productivity. When we surrender to God's will, He begins working on these things. He frees us from the destructive power of sin and the evil influences of the devil so that we can be our best for Him.

▦ **God is able to keep us from decisions and situations that diminish our potential.**

Every person is created by God with incredible potential. Just like a seed has amazing potential that is only released in the right environment, our potential is released as God places us in the proper life environments. As we walk in His will, He keeps us from making decisions and getting involved in situations that will diminish the potential He has placed in us.

▦ **God is able to release supernatural resources that enable us to live life at a heavenly level.**

Getting into the will of God is wonderful, because in His will we find a flow of supernatural provision. When we busy ourselves with becoming the person God wants us to be and fulfilling the assignments He asks us to do, God releases heavenly resources to us.

The greatest joy in all the world is found in doing

the will of God. It is worth whatever price we have to pay to discover it. Getting on this pathway with God, by learning to live daily in His will, is the most rewarding decision we will ever make.

To know God's will we must know God. The Bible tells us how to know Him in a real and intimate way:

> "For God so loved the world that he gave his only Son, so that everyone who believes in him will not perish but have eternal life" *(John 3:16)*.

> "Jesus told him, 'I am the way, the truth, and the life. No one can come to the Father except through me'" *(John 14:6)*.

> "For if you confess with your mouth that Jesus is Lord and believe in your heart that God raised him from the dead, you will be saved. For it is by believing in your heart that you are made right with God, and it is by confessing with your mouth that you are saved" *(Romans 10:9-10)*.

"Look! Here I stand at the door and knock.
If you hear me calling and open the door, I will
come in, and we will share a meal as friends"
(Revelation 3:20).

If you have never met the Lord, know that He has
a wonderful plan for your life. To discover His plan,
you need to give Him your heart. If you have not
done so, ask Him into your life right now by
sincerely praying a very simple prayer:

*"Dear Jesus, I admit that I am a sinner in need of
Your forgiveness. I am sorry for all the things I have
done wrong. I believe that You are God's Son, and that
You died on the cross for my sins. I believe that You
rose again from the dead. I ask You to come into my
life. Forgive me of all my sins. Make me a new
person. I give my life to You. Thank You for saving me.
In Jesus' name, Amen."*

The Bible says that you are now a part of God's
family—one of His children. As your Heavenly
Father, you can now confidently look to Him to
guide you in an exciting adventure in this life and a
journey into eternity.

Let's get started!

How To Know
God's Will

As I wrote this title, "How To Know God's Will," I must confess that I felt a bit presumptuous. How could I, or anyone else for that matter, attempt to tell or teach others about something as lofty and wonderful as knowing the will of God?

The truth is, God has outlined in His Word certain key steps we can take that help us discover His will. I am simply going to share with you some of what I have learned from the Bible, and from my experiences with God about finding His will.

The twelve keys I outline here are certainly not exhaustive, but I do believe they are comprehensive. They cover what I consider to be basic principles that cannot be neglected if we genuinely want God's guidance. I use these keys in my life when facing decisions and seeking God's will.

It is also important to know that, even as we take these steps we will still make mistakes in the process of seeking to know the will of God. As the Apostle Paul so clearly reminded us, "Now we see things imperfectly as in a poor mirror, but then we will see everything with perfect clarity. All that I know now is partial and incomplete, but then I will know everything completely, just as God knows me now" *(I Corinthians 13:12)*.

We view life through the lens of our earthly existence and our ongoing battle with sin and the devil. These influences mean that our sense of direction will sometimes be uncertain and our vision of what God wants for us will sometimes be fuzzy. This is part of the legacy of living in a fallen world.

It is comforting and reassuring to know that God is not looking for our perfection in every detail of knowing His will. He is interested in a heart that simply delights in Him and consistently seeks His highest and best.

With these things in mind, let's take a look at some keys to discovering God's will.

God's will is always confirmed through His Word.

God will never lead us to do anything that is contrary to the laws, instructions and spirit of the Bible—His Word. If an action or decision we are contemplating is not supported in God's Word, it must not be entertained or engaged in by us.

When seeking to know what the Bible has to say about a decision, consider:

✺ **The precepts of God's Word.**

These are the clearly defined laws and instructions God has given us. Never go down a path that God's Word has forbidden. Always follow the laws and instructions of Scripture. Let God's precepts be your guide.

✺ **The principles of God's Word.**

There are times when a particular decision or direction we are considering is not specifically addressed in the Bible. At this point, ask yourself if there are principles enfolded in

15

God's precepts or presented in principle through the stories and characters of Scripture that apply to the situation you are facing. You will be amazed how many times the principles of God's Word will guide you.

For example, when someone is considering a decision about marriage, the Bible does not specifically tell them the name or details of the person they are to marry. However, there are guiding principles in God's Word that will help them understand the kind of person God wants them to look for, and the process He wants them to use in making their decision about a mate.

⚜ The personal promises of God's Word.

One of the ways God guides us is through personal inspiration from His Word. As we prayerfully read and study our Bible, God can and will illuminate certain passages and promises that help us know what He wants us to do.

We should always be careful that our

"inspirations" from Scripture are truly scriptural—that they are consistent with the precepts and principles God has given us in His Word.

Obedience to God's Word and His revealed will are necessary for discovering more of God's will.

God expects us to live in obedience to His Word. Disobedience to God's Word will keep us from getting guidance from God. He also expects us to faithfully fulfill the placements and assignments He has already given us.

God is not inclined to give us more information about our future unless we are currently seeking to become the person He wants us to be, and are actively doing what we already know He wants us to do.

If we are not doing what God has already instructed us to do today, we should not expect Him to give us additional insight, guidance or direction for tomorrow.

God's will is understood, embraced and released through a consistent commitment to prayer.

A vibrant, consistent and persistent prayer life is essential to knowing God's will. Prayer synchronizes our heart with God's heart. In prayer we begin to understand what God wants for us. In prayer we are given the power to embrace what God wants for us. In prayer we literally release the will of God into our lives.

We see the importance of prayer in knowing the will of God through Jesus' greatest teaching on prayer. In the Lord's Prayer Jesus said, "This, then, is how you should pray...Your kingdom come, your will be done on earth as it is in heaven" *(Matthew 6:9-10 NIV)*.

Jesus practiced this kind of prayer. In the Garden of Gethsemane Jesus prayerfully embraced His Heavenly Father's plan to send Him to the cross, even though it was difficult to do so. Prayer clarified God's will for Jesus and empowered Him to do it. Prayer does the same for us.

19

We cannot fully understand, embrace and release the will of God into our lives without developing a meaningful practice of prayer.

God's will is discovered through the help of godly people.

God places people in our lives to help us in the process of discovering His will. Seeking out the right people, gaining the benefit of their counsel and wisdom is an important part of knowing what God wants us to do.

There are four characteristics of people who will be helpful to us in the process of finding God's will. They must be:

◉ **Spiritually and emotionally mature.**

Seek guidance from people who have walked with and grown in Jesus over a long period of time—people whose lifestyle and personal character reflect real spirituality. Seek help from people who are also emotionally mature—their life is stable and settled.

◉ **Objective.**

It is important to find people who are objective—not ruled by their personal opinions or feelings, or controlled by a personal agenda that might influence their input to us.

❀ Caring.

The best help in finding God's will comes from people who truly love and care for us. It is this love and care that earns them the privilege of giving us their input. People who really care about us will share their heart in loving and honest ways that help us, not hurt us.

❀ Committed.

When seeking counsel from others, seek out those who have demonstrated a commitment to you. Their commitment enables you to trust their input and advice.

When making major life decisions, it is also valuable to seek input from those God has placed in positions of authority over us. If you are a young person, or a young adult, desire, seek out and carefully consider the advice of your parents.

My advice to married couples is that they should

never make major decisions or pursue a new direction without a significant level of agreement. If something is God's will, you can trust Him to bring agreement and resolution between you and your spouse.

God's will is discovered through the wisdom of previous experiences.

All of us have certain successes and failures under our belt. We have lived a portion of life, and hopefully have learned some valuable lessons along the way. It is amazing how many people never stop, reflect and draw on the wisdom of previous experiences when facing present decisions.

What has life taught you? Where have you been successful, fruitful and fulfilled in the past? What have you learned about yourself from these experiences that apply to the decision or direction you are currently contemplating? What mistakes have you made in the past that you should be especially careful not to repeat?

God uses the wisdom of our previous experiences to help us discover the present plan He has for us.

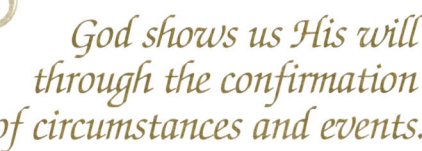

God shows us His will through the confirmation of circumstances and events.

When we are seeking God's will, we can trust Him to work in our world in ways we can see. God can and will orchestrate divine circumstances that help confirm what He wants us to do. He can and will open and close doors in the process of guiding us.

The Apostle Paul experienced this in his ministry. During one of his evangelistic campaigns, Paul repeatedly sought to go into different places to preach, and consistently ran into closed doors. He recognized these closed doors as the voice and guidance of the Holy Spirit helping him to know God's will.

As Paul continued to pray, God revealed His direction to him: "That night Paul had a vision. He saw a man from Macedonia in northern Greece, pleading with him, 'Come over here and help us.' So we decided to leave for Macedonia at once, for we could only conclude that God was calling us to preach the Good News there" *(Acts 16:9-10)*.

God was active in Paul's ministry, guiding and directing circumstances and events in his life. He will do the same for us.

A word of caution is in order here. We should never decide God's will only on the basis of perceived favorable or unfavorable circumstances and events. Too much can be read into these situations.

When we are eager to follow a particular course, or are resistant to some request or assignment God may have for us, we can look for and find circumstances and events that reinforce and confirm our predetermined desires and decision. I have observed people using the "evidence" of circumstances to convince themselves, and to try and convince others, that they were doing God's will, when in reality it was their will at work.

Circumstances and events should always be read in the light of the other steps necessary for receiving God's guidance.

*God uses the influence
of sanctified personal passion
to help us know what is best.*

Passion is a word that is often related to romance, and rightly so. Passion is the reflection and response of a person's heart and emotions to someone or something they love.

One of the ways God helps us discover His will is by sanctifying our passions, and then using them to help us find our place in life and in His Kingdom.

When people request my help in finding God's will, I usually ask them some questions about their passion. I want to know what they really love to do. I inquire as to whether there is any evidence that God has blessed this passion in the past. I am interested in finding out what others think about their perceived areas of passion.

For example, someone may say to me that they are passionate about music. Unless their musical ability is affirmed by others, and unless there is clear evidence that God blesses and anoints this expression in their lives, I certainly would not encourage them to "follow their passion," quit their job, sell their house, pack their bags and move to Nashville!

Our passions give us clues as to what God wants us to do, but they cannot be analyzed and pursued in a vacuum. They must be submitted to the tests of affirmation and confirmation by God and others.

Discovering God's will requires patience.

One of the great things about God is that He is never in a hurry. He is willing to wait. He wants us to be willing to wait also. This is not an easy thing to do.

All too often we rush into situations without prayerfully and carefully considering our course. The result is that we usually find ourselves in a major mess, asking God to rescue us.

It is a lot easier to patiently pray and wait for God's guidance on the front end of a decision than it is to cry out in pain for His help and deliverance once a significant mistake has been made because of our impatience.

Waiting on God is always worth it. Waiting time need not be wasted time. As we patiently wait for God's guidance, we cultivate our character by being faithful where He has us.

Many times this waiting time is really a testing time. God is checking out the condition of our heart. He is watching us to see if we will stay submitted to Him, even when we don't fully understand all He is doing. He is working to build our trust in Him.

Be willing to humbly and patiently wait on God's will to be revealed before you move forward. Very seldom have I regretted waiting to make a major decision. Quite frequently I have regretted impatience and impulsiveness!

*To find God's will
we must possess a spirit
of gratitude, not grumbling.*

God is drawn to praise-filled, positive people. He likes to associate with people of gratitude. It is one of the qualities that attract God's attention.

People who are grateful for where they are, and for what they have, are better positioned for getting guidance from God. Grumblers are so preoccupied with the negative that they cannot see or appreciate the blessings already surrounding them. Seeing and appreciating the good things we have is crucial to receiving more from God.

The Bible declares that a spirit of gratitude is God's will for us: "No matter what happens, always be thankful, for this is God's will for you who belong to Christ Jesus" *(I Thessalonians 5:18)*.

Lots of believers are experiencing less than God's best because they have never confronted and conquered their grumbling spirit. Grumbling cost an entire generation of Israelites their place in the Promised Land. It is costly to us also.

31

Discovering God's will requires a spirit of faith, not fear.

Faith is another quality that attracts God's attention. Faith is something we need if we are going to be led by the Lord. Fear paralyzes and immobilizes us. Faith activates us. It causes us to reach out to God for the next step and plan He has for us, even when all the details of His plan are not yet clear.

I grew up in church and became a Christian when I was seven years old. One of the things I remember about my early spiritual pilgrimage is my fear of God's will.

My immature concept was that surrendering to God's will usually involved being required to do something very hard and unpleasant. I was sure that, if I ever prayed for God's will to be done in my life, He surely would send me to some far-flung, undeveloped country where I would have to eat horrible food and live a dreadful, joyless life.

As ridiculous as this seems, there are a lot of

"grown-up" believers who operate with the same concept. They live in fear of what God might ask them to do. They have drawn tight boundaries around their lives defining what they are willing to say yes to, should God come calling.

As you can imagine, this mindset of fear restricts us from being open to all God has for us. It keeps us in the driver's seat, instead of giving God total control and prerogative over our will and plans.

To find the fullness of God's will, we must be done with fearing the will of God. Our faith needs to be in our Heavenly Father who loves us and is good. He always wants the best for us. Our faith needs to take hold of the many wonderful promises He provides us in His Word.

God's will always involves a "calling to," not a "running from."

This is an important principle to remember. Many people make decisions to leave something behind and move on to something new out of discontentment and frustration. They are "running from" a situation. In this process many Christians "blame" their decision on God's guidance.

I have discovered that God does not endorse our irresponsibility. He does not condone our choices to run from things that are designed to make us more mature. If discontentment and frustration are our primary reasons for making a change, a move or a certain decision, we are missing the mark.

When seeking God's will, especially in relationship to a major change, move or decision, it is always important to prayerfully ask the question, "Am I responding to a call from God to something new, or am I running from something God is trying to do in my life?"

God's will is affirmed by the presence of God's peace.

As we follow these keys to God's guidance outlined in His Word, we can be sure that God will not leave us without an inner witness— something on the inside that affirms His will. That something is His peace.

One of the ways we know that we are in the will of God is the attending peace of God in our hearts.

This doesn't mean that living in God's will is always easy or problem-free. In fact, sometimes the will of God leads through valleys, trials and tough times. Nevertheless, as we faithfully walk in God's will we can always go back to the place of peace, knowing that we are doing what He wants us to do, where He wants us to do it.

The Apostle Paul reminded us of this ingredient in knowing the will of God: "The peace that Christ gives is to guide you in the decisions you make; for it is to this peace that God has called you

together in the one body. And be thankful"
(Colossians 3:15 TEV).

God wants us to know His will. As we follow the keys He has given us in His Word, we can be assured of His guidance.

Join me in this prayer:

"Dear Lord, I know that You love me more than I can imagine. I know that Your will represents Your best for my life. Today I pray for Your Kingdom to come and Your will to be done in my life. Forgive me for any past resistance to Your will. I choose to fully cooperate with You as You continue to lead my life. In Jesus' name, Amen."

Scriptural Promises
And Instructions For
Discovering God's Will

II Samuel 5:23a
And once again David asked the LORD what to do....

✝— —✝

Psalm 23
The LORD is my shepherd; I have everything I need. He lets me rest in green meadows; he leads me beside peaceful streams. He renews my strength. He guides me along right paths, bringing honor to his name. Even when I walk through the dark valley of death, I will not be afraid, for you are close beside me. Your rod and your staff protect and comfort me. You prepare a feast for me in the presence of my enemies. You welcome me as a guest, anointing my head with oil. My cup overflows with blessings. Surely your goodness and unfailing love will pursue me all the days of my life, and I will live in the house of the LORD forever.

✝— —✝

Psalm 25:9
He leads the humble in what is right, teaching them his way.

✝— —✝

Psalm 32:8
The LORD says, "I will guide you along the best pathway for your life. I will advise you and watch over you."

Psalm 37:7
Be still before the LORD and wait patiently for him; do not fret when men succeed in their ways, when they carry out their wicked schemes.

Psalm 119:105
Your word is a lamp for my feet and a light for my path.

Psalm 143:10
Teach me to do your will, for you are my God. May your gracious Spirit lead me forward on a firm footing.

Proverbs 3:5, 6
Trust in the LORD with all your heart; do not depend on your own understanding. Seek his will in all you do, and he will direct your paths.

Proverbs 4:11
I will teach you wisdom's ways and lead you in straight paths.

Proverbs 12:26
The godly give good advice to their friends; the wicked lead them astray.

Matthew 6:9, 10
Pray like this: Our Father in heaven, may your name be honored. May your Kingdom come soon. May your will be done here on earth, just as it is in heaven.

Matthew 7:7, 8
Keep on asking, and you will be given what you ask for. Keep on looking, and you will find. Keep on knocking, and the door will be opened. For everyone who asks, receives. Everyone who seeks, finds. And the door is opened to everyone who knocks.

Matthew 26:36-42

Then Jesus brought them to an olive grove called Gethsemane, and he said, "Sit here while I go on ahead to pray." He took Peter and Zebedee's two sons, James and John, and he began to be filled with anguish and deep distress. He told them, "My soul is crushed with grief to the point of death. Stay here and watch with me." He went on a little farther and fell face down on the ground, praying, "My Father! If it is possible, let this cup of suffering be taken away from me. Yet I want your will, not mine." Then he returned to the disciples and found them asleep. He said to Peter, "Couldn't you stay awake and watch with me even one hour? Keep alert and pray. Otherwise temptation will overpower you. For though the spirit is willing enough, the body is weak!" Again he left them and prayed, "My Father! If this cup cannot be taken away until I drink it, your will be done."

John 4:34

Then Jesus explained: "My nourishment comes from doing the will of God, who sent me, and from finishing his work."

John 10:10
The thief's purpose is to steal and kill and destroy.
My purpose is to give life in all its fullness.

Acts 16:9, 10
That night Paul had a vision. He saw a man from
Macedonia in northern Greece, pleading with him,
"Come over here and help us." So we decided to
leave for Macedonia at once, for we could only
conclude that God was calling us to preach the
Good News there.

I Corinthians 13:12
Now we see things imperfectly as in a poor
mirror, but then we will see everything with
perfect clarity. All that I know now is partial and
incomplete, but then I will know everything
completely, just as God knows me now.

Ephesians 1:15-18
Ever since I first heard of your strong faith
in the Lord Jesus and your love for Christians
everywhere, I have never stopped thanking God
for you. I pray for you constantly, asking God, the

glorious Father of our Lord Jesus Christ, to give you spiritual wisdom and understanding, so that you might grow in your knowledge of God. I pray that your hearts will be flooded with light so that you can understand the wonderful future he has promised to those he called. I want you to realize what a rich and glorious inheritance he has given to his people.

Colossians 1:9-10
So we have continued praying for you ever since we first heard about you. We ask God to give you a complete understanding of what he wants to do in your lives, and we ask him to make you wise with spiritual wisdom. Then the way you live will always honor and please the Lord, and you will continually do good, kind things for others. All the while, you will learn to know God better and better.

Colossians 2:6
So then, just as you received Christ Jesus as Lord, continue to live in him.

Colossians 3:15
And let the peace that comes from Christ rule in your hearts. For as members of one body you are all called to live in peace. And always be thankful.

+≡= =≡+

I Thessalonians 5:18
No matter what happens, always be thankful, for this is God's will for you who belong to Christ Jesus.

+≡= =≡+

II Timothy 1:7
For God has not given us a spirit of fear and timidity, but of power, love, and self-discipline.

+≡= =≡+

II Timothy 2: 21
If you keep yourself pure, you will be a utensil God can use for his purpose. Your life will be clean, and you will be ready for the Master to use you for every good work.

+≡= =≡+

James 1:5, 6
If you need wisdom-if you want to know what God wants you to do-ask him, and he will gladly tell you. He will not resent your asking. But when you ask

him, be sure that you really expect him to answer, for a doubtful mind is as unsettled as a wave of the sea that is driven and tossed by the wind.